SCHIRMER'S LIBRARY
OF MUSICAL CLASSICS

Vol. 2144

EDVARD GRIEG

Easier Lyric Pieces
for Piano

ISBN 978-1-5400-4210-1

G. SCHIRMER, *Inc.*

DISTRIBUTED BY

www.halleonard.com

Contact us:
Hal Leonard
7777 West Bluemound Road
Milwaukee, WI 53213
Email: info@halleonard.com

In Europe, contact:
Hal Leonard Europe Limited
42 Wigmore Street
Marylebone, London, W1U 2RN
Email: info@halleonardeurope.com

In Australia, contact:
Hal Leonard Australia Pty. Ltd.
4 Lentara Court
Cheltenham, Victoria, 3192 Australia
Email: info@halleonard.com.au

CONTENTS

Arietta
from *Lyric Pieces*

Edvard Grieg
Op. 12, No. 1

Poco Andante e sostenuto

Waltz
in A minor
from *Lyric Pieces*

Edvard Grieg
Op. 12, No. 2

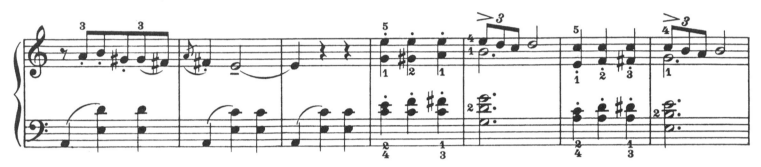

Coda

Watchman's Song
from *Lyric Pieces*

Edvard Grieg
Op. 12, No. 3

Molto Andante e semplice

Intermezzo

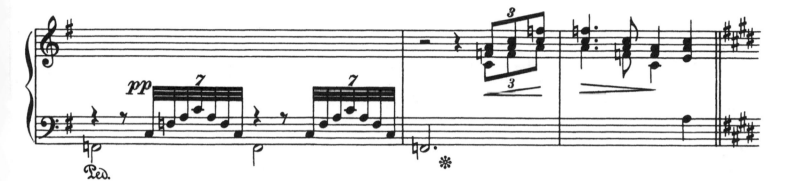

Elves' Dance

from *Lyric Pieces*

Edvard Grieg
Op. 12, No. 4

Molto Allegro e sempre staccato

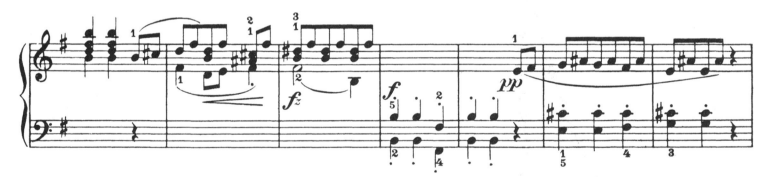

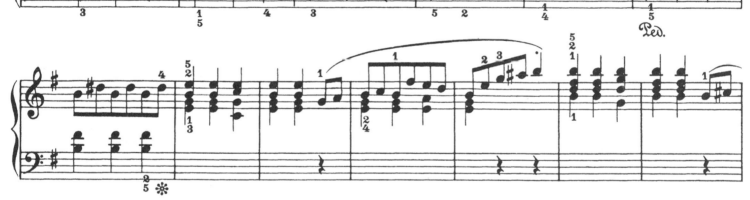

Norwegian Melody
from *Lyric Pieces*

Edvard Grieg
Op. 12, No. 6

Presto marcato

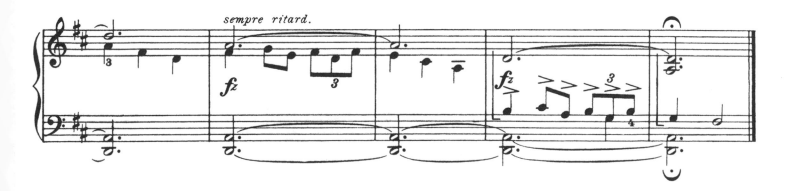

National Song

from *Lyric Pieces*

Edvard Grieg
Op. 12, No. 8

Maestoso

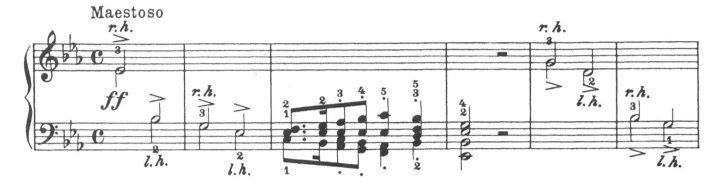

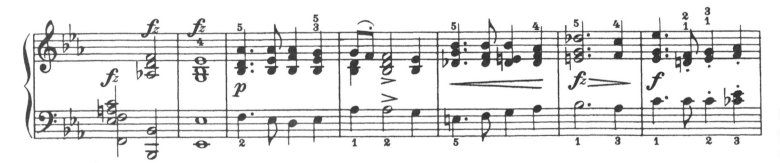

Berceuse

from *Lyric Pieces*

Edvard Grieg
Op. 38, No. 1

Con moto

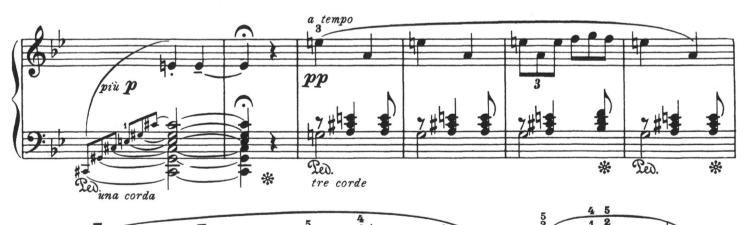

Popular Melody

from *Lyric Pieces*

Edvard Grieg
Op. 38, No. 2

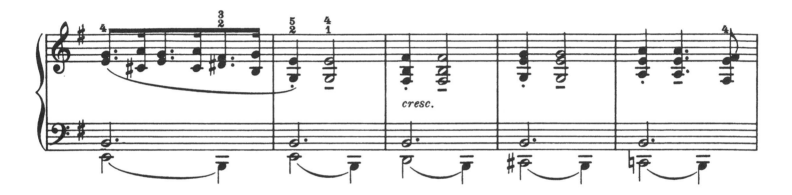

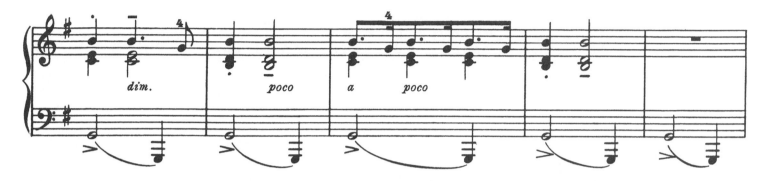

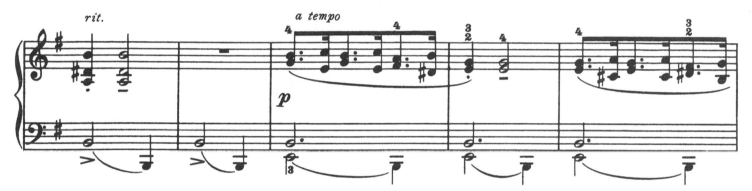

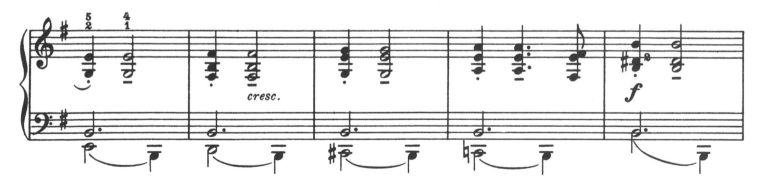

Spring Dance

from *Lyric Pieces*

Edvard Grieg
Op. 38, No. 5

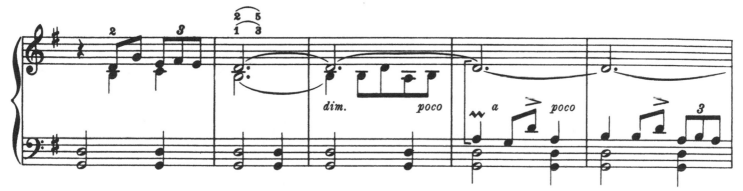

Waltz
in E minor
from *Lyric Pieces*

Edvard Grieg
Op. 38, No. 7

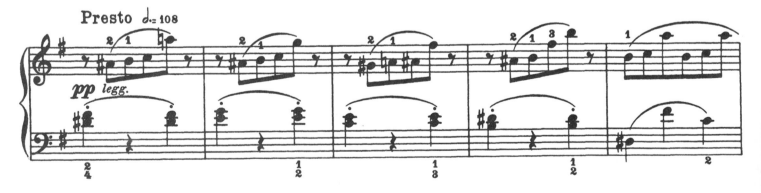

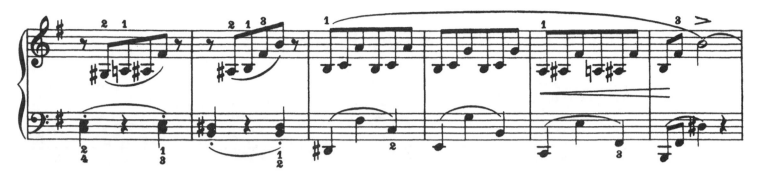

Tempo I

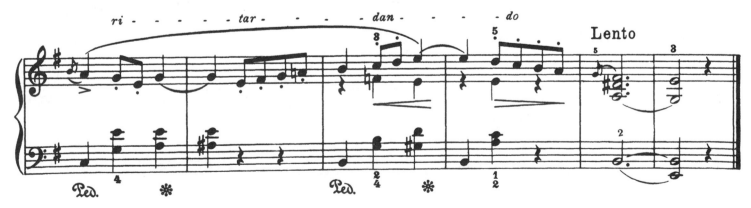

Little Bird
from *Lyric Pieces*

Edvard Grieg
Op. 43, No. 4

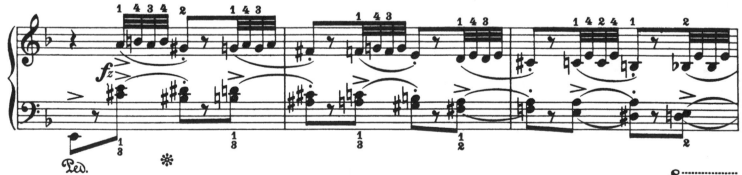

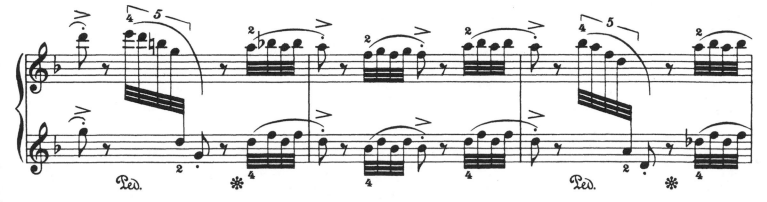

poco ritar - - - dan - - - - do

Notturno

from *Lyric Pieces*

Edvard Grieg
Op. 54, No. 4

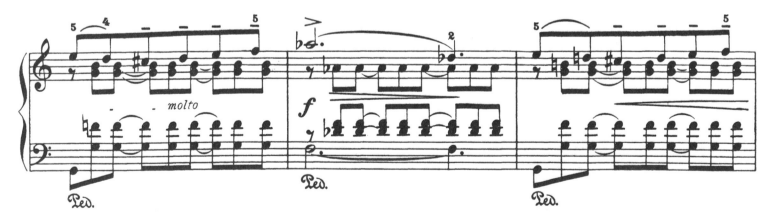

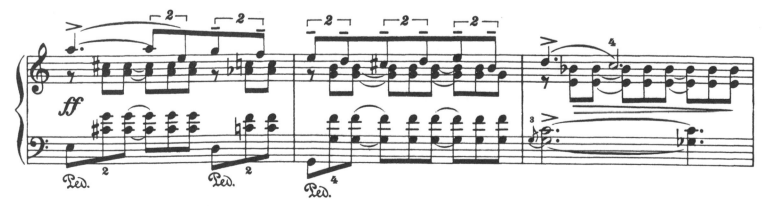

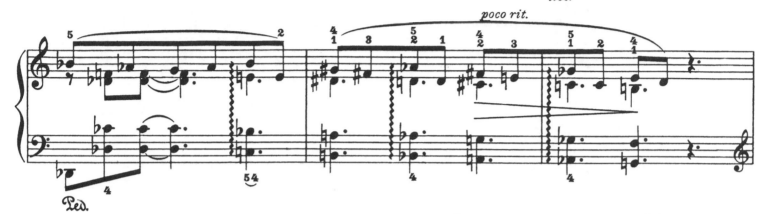

Bell Ringing

from *Lyric Pieces*

Edvard Grieg
Op. 54, No. 6

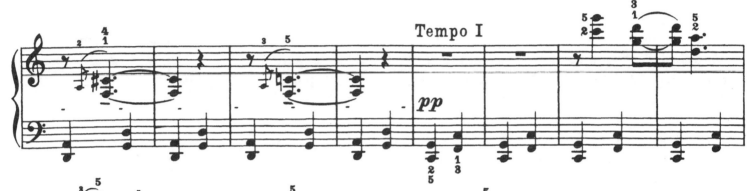

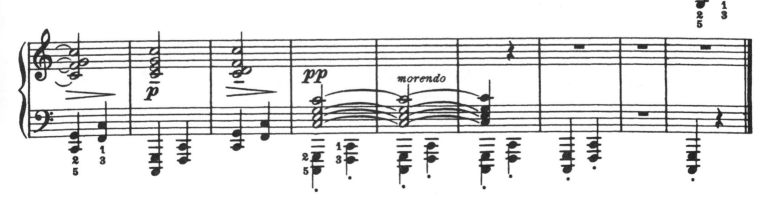

French Serenade

from *Lyric Pieces*

Edvard Grieg
Op. 62, No. 3

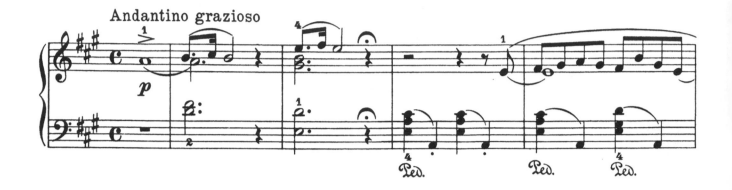

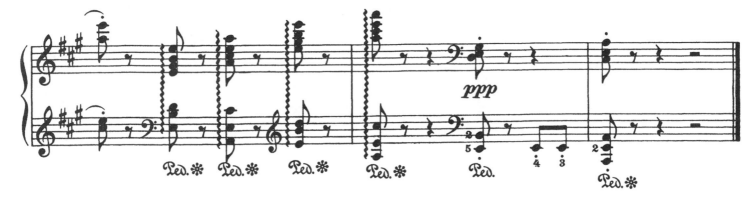

Phantom

from *Lyric Pieces*

Edvard Grieg
Op. 62, No. 5

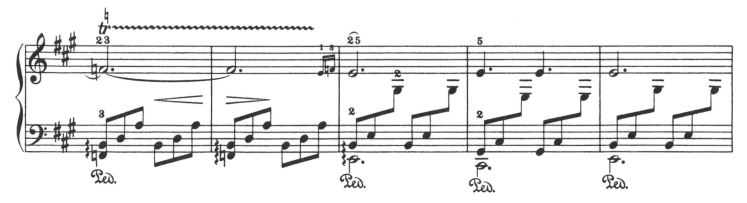

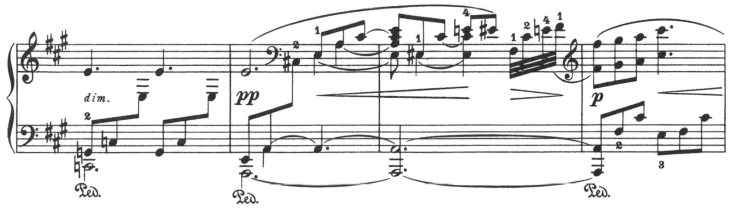

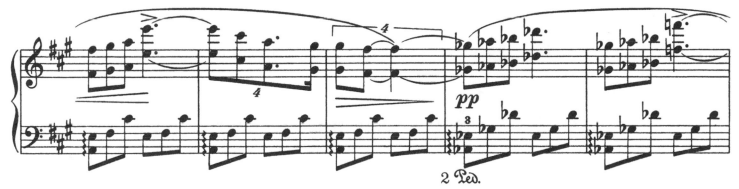

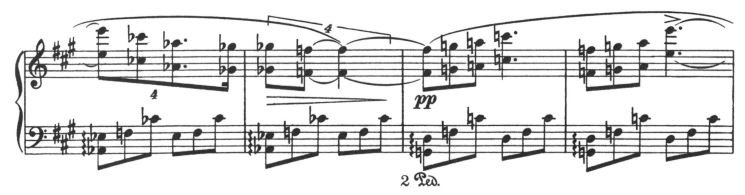

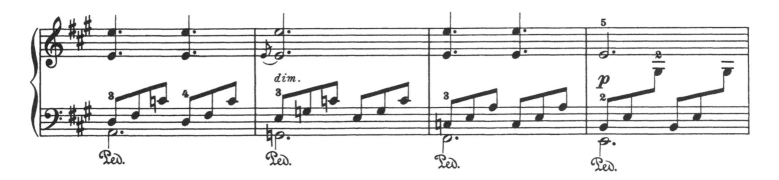

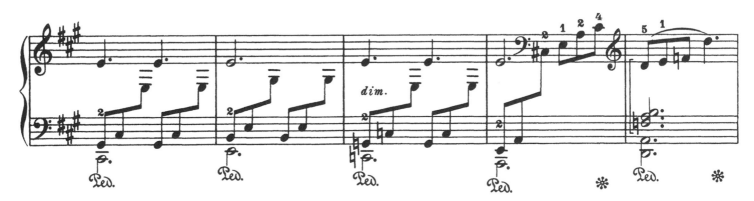

Puck

from *Lyric Pieces*

Edvard Grieg
Op. 71, No. 3

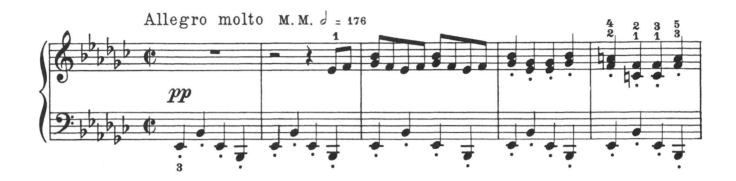

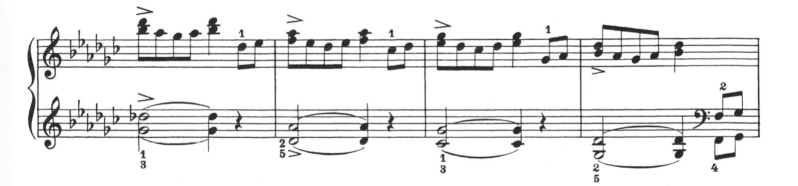

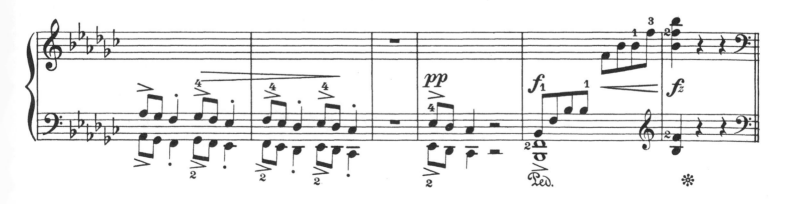

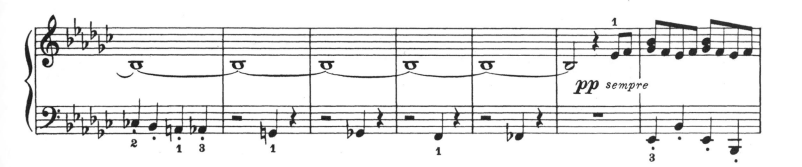

Peasant's Song

from *Lyric Pieces*

Edvard Grieg
Op. 65, No. 2

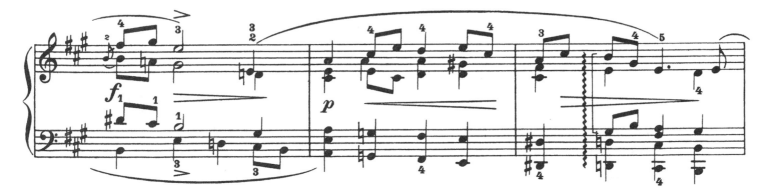

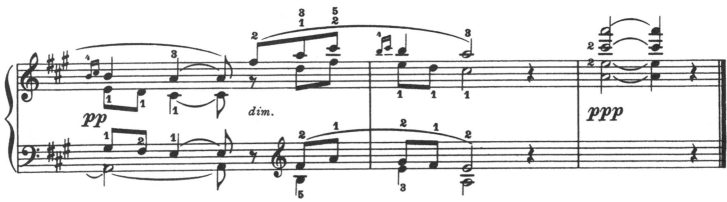

Sailor's Song

from *Lyric Pieces*

Edvard Grieg
Op. 68, No. 1

Allegro vivace e marcato

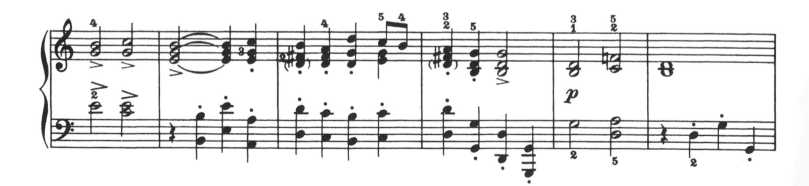

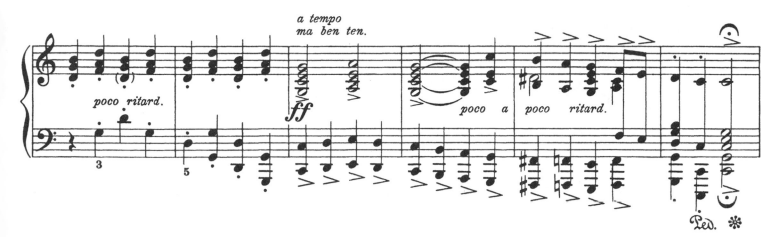

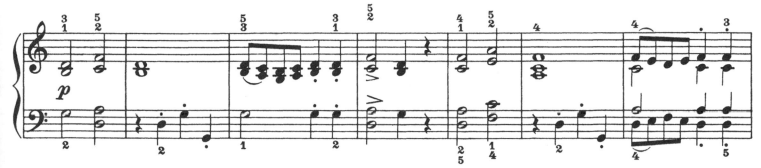

Grandmother's Minuet

from *Lyric Pieces*

Edvard Grieg
Op. 68, No. 2

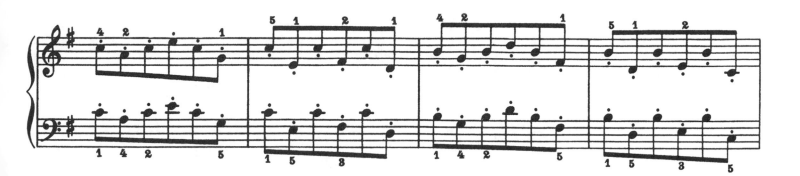

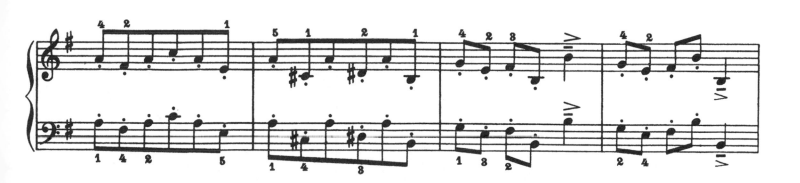

At Your Feet

from *Lyric Pieces*

Edvard Grieg
Op. 68, No. 3

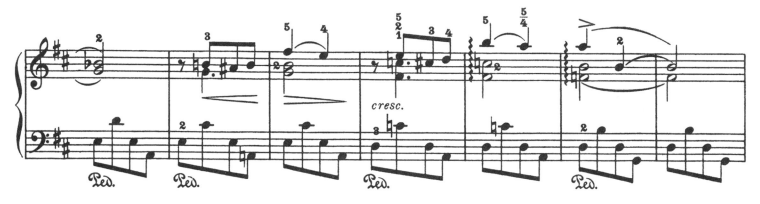

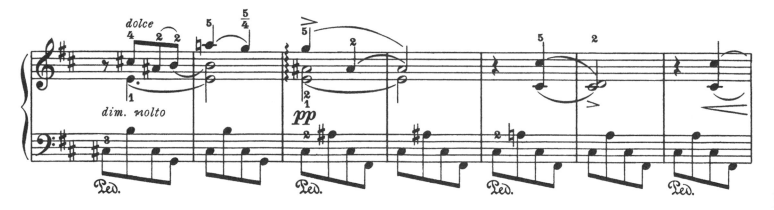

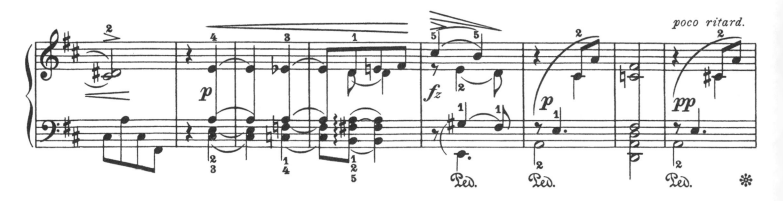

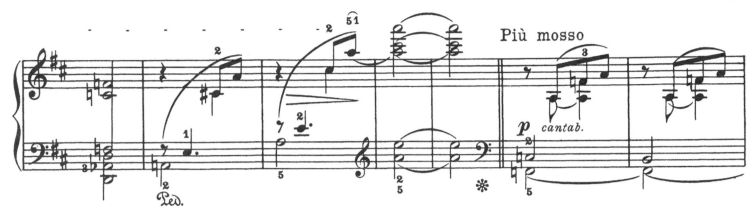

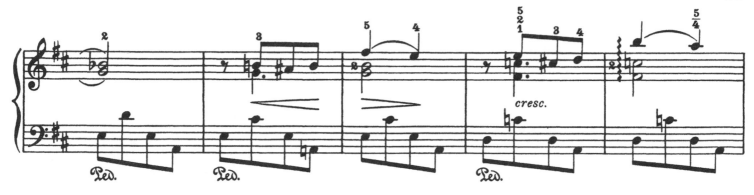

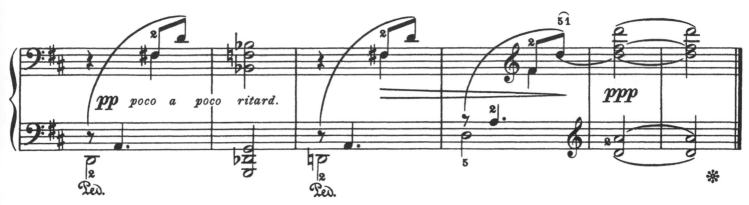

Evening in the Mountains

from *Lyric Pieces*

Edvard Grieg
Op. 68, No. 4

Tempo I

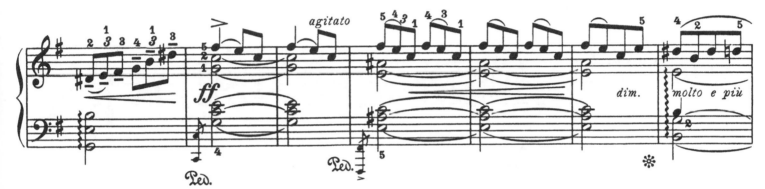

Cradle Song

from *Lyric Pieces*

Edvard Grieg
Op. 68, No. 5

Allegretto tranquillamente

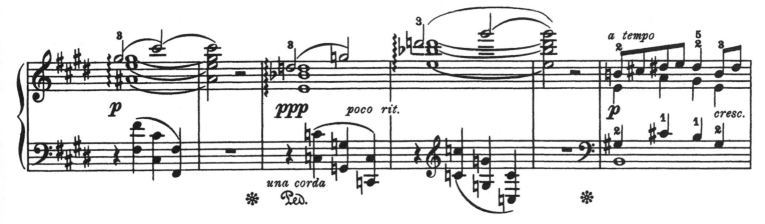

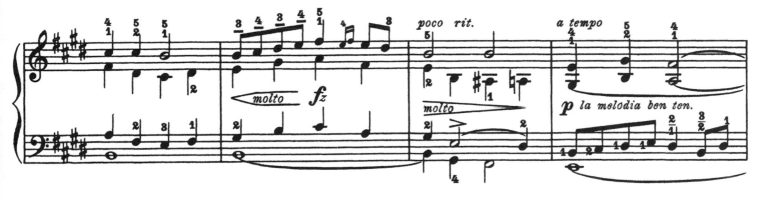

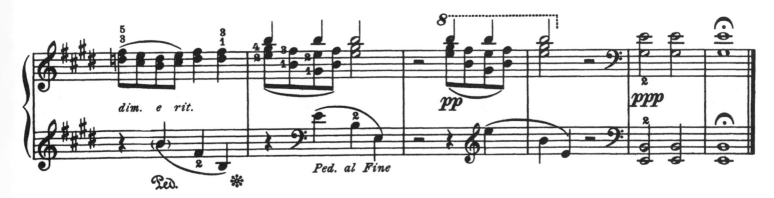

Gone

from *Lyric Pieces*

Edvard Grieg
Op. 71, No. 6

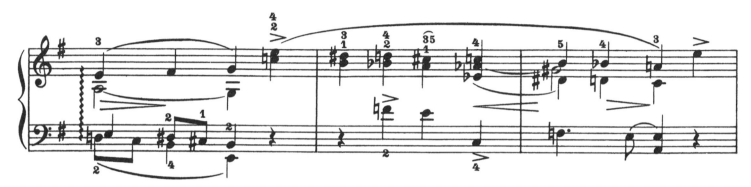

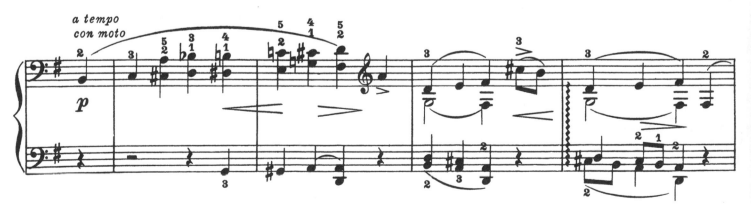

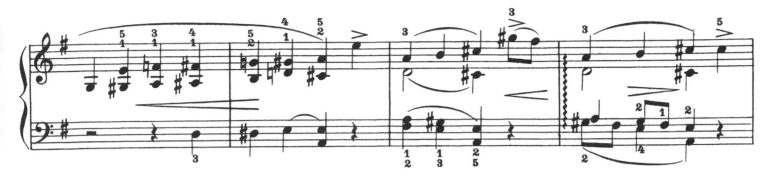

Remembrances

from *Lyric Pieces*

Edvard Grieg
Op. 71, No. 7

Tempo di Valse

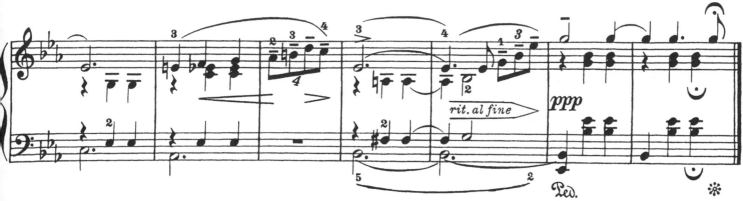

Ballad

from *Lyric Pieces*

Edvard Grieg
Op. 65, No. 5

Op. 65, No. 5

Lento lugubre

Tempo I

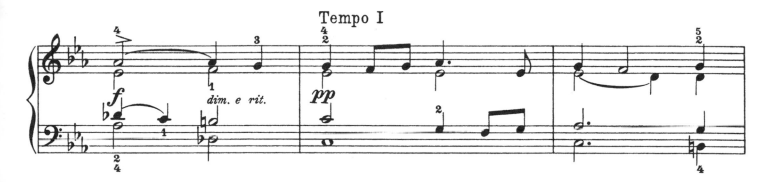

Tempo I